BOXING SKILLS

The Diagram Group

BROCKHAMPTON
DIAGRAM
GUIDES

Boxing Skills

© Diagram Visual Information Ltd. 1997
195 Kentish Town Road
London
NW5 2JU

First published in Great Britain in 1997 by
Brockhampton Press Ltd
20 Bloomsbury Street
London
WC1 2QA
a member of the Hodder Headline Group PLC

ISBN 1-86019-809-0

Also in this series:
Calligraphy
Card Games
Chinese Astrology
Drawing People
How the Body Works
Identifying Architecture
Kings and Queens of Britain
Magic Tricks
Origami
Party Games
Pub Games
SAS Survival Skills
Soccer Skills
Understanding Heraldry
World History

Introduction

Boxing has been around in one form or another for thousands of years. Today it is a fast, professional and exciting sport which is followed by millions all around the world. Great title fights have become legendary events and great boxers are modern-day heroes. *Boxing Skills* is a complete introductory guide to the sport. Within this book are sections dealing with everything from rules and equipment to fighting and training techniques. Whether you want to take part or just enjoy as a spectator *Boxing Skills* will provide you with a wealth of facts, tips and essential information about the art of pugilism. *Boxing Skills* is illustrated throughout with easy-to-follow diagrams which are closely linked to the clear, explanatory text.

Contents

6	Boxing today
7	Basics of boxing
14	Rules of boxing
20	A boxing match
23	Fighting techniques
38	Training techniques
44	Glossary

Boxing today

Boxing today is a highly skilled contest between trained athletes. The modern form of the sport, with competitors wearing gloves, has its origins in a set of rules laid down in 1865 by the Marquess of Queensberry, known as the Queensberry Rules. These were formulated to regulate the popular form of gloved fighting which began to replace bare knuckle, or prize, fighting in the mid-19th century.

Prize fighting was more a test of endurance than skill. Exhausted and bloodied fighters could slog away at each other for hours until one or other succumbed to his injuries or sheer fatigue. On one occasion a prize fight went to 185 rounds and lasted over six hours! Once gloves began to be worn the style of the sport changed rapidly. Gloves were introduced to protect the hands rather than give added weight to the punches, and, in fact, lessen the weight of the blows. Consequently fighters had to develop defensive skills and more subtle tactics.

The mental and physical agility required of the modern boxer is a direct result of the changes introduced under the Queensberry Rules. Today, successful boxers also have to cope with the added problems of celebrity status and the relentless pressure to win created by the huge cash prizes at stake.

If you want to see whether you enjoy boxing, and have any talent for it, ask your gym teacher at school about lessons or join a youth club which offers tuition. You won't become a boxer overnight; as with all sports it takes dedication and hours of training in the basic techniques. You will also have to develop a high level of physical fitness and mental concentration if you want to succeed.

Basics of boxing

AMATEUR OR PROFESSIONAL

In most countries there are two basic forms of boxing: amateur and professional. The techniques and rules for both are more or less identical, but only professional boxers can fight for money prizes. Most boxers begin in amateur contests. Controlling organisations, such as the Amateur Boxing Association in Great Britain and the Amateur Athletic Union in the United States, run national competitions and select teams for international contests. Only amateur boxers are allowed to compete in the Olympic Games.

DRESS AND EQUIPMENT

Clothes Amateur boxers wear shorts and vests. Professionals wear shorts only.

Gloves Professional and amateur boxers wear 230g (8oz) gloves up to welterweight and 280g (10oz) gloves above welterweight.

Bandages/Bindings Boxers wind long lengths of bandage around their hands to protect them from the impact of punching. Amateurs may use 2.5m (8ft 2in) of 5cm (2in) wide soft dry bandage, or 2m (6ft 6in) of Velpeau dry bandage, on each hand. Professionals above middleweight may use 5.5m (18ft) of 5cm (2in) wide dry bandage, or 3.3m (11ft) of 2.5cm (1in) wide zinc oxide tape. Professionals below middleweight are allowed 2.75m (9ft) of dry bandage. Professionals may use bandages and tapes. Bandages may be wound over the knuckles but tape must stop 1.25cm ($^1/_2$in) from the knuckles.

Gumshield All boxers wear a thick plastic guard shaped to fit around their teeth. This prevents them from accidentally biting their tongue when punched.

Boots Lightweight boots with flexible rubber soles give a boxer good grip in the ring and also support his ankles.

Socks Worn inside boots to prevent rubbing, usually extend over top of boots.

Protector Guards vulnerable genital areas from low punches.

Headguard Amateur boxers wear a headguard similar to the ones used in sparring. These make knockout punches, and the damage they can cause, less likely.

1 Shorts
2 Vest
3 Gloves
4 Bandages
5 Gumshield
6 Boots
7 Socks
8 Protector
9 Headguard

Professional   **Amateur**

TARGET AREA

To score points in a boxing match, punches must strike the target area and impact with the correct part of the glove. The target area covers the front and sides of the head and the body above the belt. Good punches impact with the knuckle part of the glove.

Target area

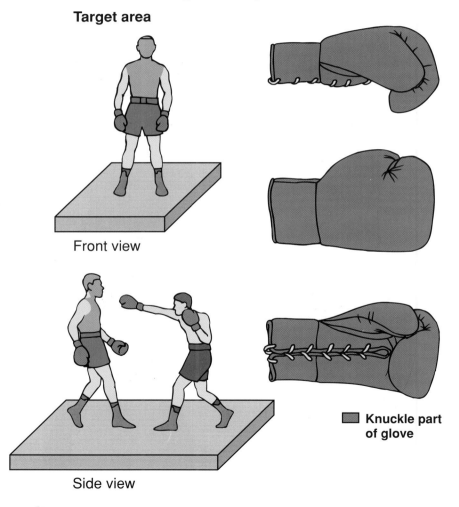

Front view

Side view

█ **Knuckle part of glove**

VULNERABILITIES

Certain parts of the body are particularly vulnerable to punches. These are: the chin, the heart and the solar plexus. The basic guard-up position is designed to protect these areas above all. Other areas of the body are even more vulnerable to punches; these include the groin, the back of the neck and the kidneys. It is strictly against the rules to punch in any of these areas.

Vulnerable areas
1 Chin
2 Heart
3 Solar plexus

Punches against the rules

Back of the neck

The kidneys

© DIAGRAM

GOOD BOXING (1)

A successful boxer must be able to move quickly as well
as hit hard. More boxing bouts are won with the feet than
the fists. It is vital to be able to keep out of reach of an
opponent's punches.

TACTICS (2)

Different boxers have different strengths and weaknesses.
A very tall boxer may have the advantage of reach and
power, but may be too slow to defend himself at close
quarters. Boxers must develop tactics for dealing with all
types of opponents. You must learn to use your own
strengths and exploit your opponent's weaknesses.

SECONDS (3)

Although every boxer fights alone, he always has trusted seconds to back him up. Between rounds, his seconds will offer advice on tactics, give encouragement and attend to any injuries.

SPORTSMANSHIP (4)

Always remember that boxing is a sport and not a free-for-all. Treat your opponent with respect, fight fairly and obey the rules. Even in the heat of a close contest you must never hit an opponent when he is down or be tempted to deliver an illegal blow.

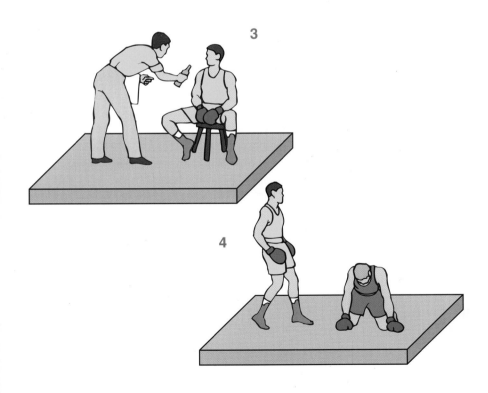

Rules of boxing

Boxing is a tough physical sport. Strict rules exist to ensure fairness and prevent unnecessary injury. These rules cover every aspect of a contest. They are laid down and enforced by the national and international organisations which govern boxing.

THE RING

Professional contests are held in a ring between 4.9m (16ft) and 6.7m (22ft) square. Amateur rings are between 4.3m (14ft) and 6.1m (20ft) square. The ring is bounded by three ropes, although in some amateur contests only two ropes are used. The floor of the ring is made of canvas with a felt or rubber underlay. The floor space must extend 46cm (1ft 6in) beyond the ropes.

OFFICIALS

In both amateur and professional contests the following officials must be present.

Referee He has complete control over, and responsibility for, everything that happens inside the ring. In particular he ensures that the fight is fair and that both boxers conform to the rules. He also makes sure that the boxers are properly dressed and that nobody other than their designated seconds attends them between rounds. A referee can issue cautions to a boxer who commits fouls and, in extreme cases, can disqualify a boxer for persistently breaking the rules. He can also stop a fight at any time if he feels that a boxer is in danger of permanent or serious injury.

Judges There are 3 in amateur and professional contests.

(Olympic and world games have 5.) They award points based on a boxer's performance which can be used to decide the result of a bout. In England the referee is the sole judge of a professional contest in all bouts including title fights under BBBC rules.

Timekeeper Ensures that every round and the time between rounds is of the right duration. He rings a bell to indicate the start and end of every round.

Doctor Present at every fight. Provides medical treatment, and also assesses a fighter's condition if the referee feels one of the fighters is too injured to continue.

The ring and officials

1 Referee
2 Judges
3 Timekeeper
4 Official seconds
5 Boxers

FOULS

Many rules exist in boxing which prohibit certain kinds of punches or other physical contacts. Blows which break these rules are called fouls. They include punching below the belt (**1**), on the back of the neck (**2**) and over the kidneys (**3**). Pivot or back-hand blows are also fouls, as are blows with the butt of the hand (**4**), the wrist, the elbow (**5**) or the inside of the glove (**6**). Excessive body contact, shouldering, head butting (**7**) and wrestling are also illegal. Other fouls include persistently ducking below the waist line (**8**); failing to break from a clinch; holding onto the ropes; and striking an opponent on a break, when he is falling or when he is on the floor (**9**). The referee may rule as a foul any act which he considers to be against the rules. Fouls are punishable by cautions, which result in a loss of points, or even by disqualification.

GOVERNING BODIES

The Amateur Boxing Association (ABA), founded in 1880 in London, was the first body to organise boxing. The world championships are held at the Olympic Games, a stepping stone for many to professional careers. A notable example is that of Muhammad Ali, who as Cassius Clay won the gold medal in 1960 at light-heavyweight level. Other championships occur between the Olympic Games.

In 1920, the National Boxing Association (NBA) was set up in the USA; it became the World Boxing Association (WBA) in 1962. The British Boxing Board of Control (BBBC) was founded in 1929. The WBA, the World Boxing Council (WBC) (founded in 1963), the World Boxing Organisation (WBO) (founded in 1988) and the International Boxing Federation (IBF) (founded in 1983) all disagree on regulations, so each runs its own championships. With up to 17 professional weight categories and 12 Olympic and amateur weights, there are a maximum of 80 different world champions at any one time.

Boxers take on opponents of comparable weight. The various WBC weight divisions are shown opposite.

WBC weight categories		Amateur		Professional	
		lb	kg	lb	kg
Strawweight (Mini flyweight)	up to	–	–	105	47.7
Light flyweight (Junior flyweight)	up to	105.8	48	108	49
Flyweight	up to	112.4	51	112	50.8
Super flyweight (Junior bantamweight)	up to	–	–	115	52.2
Bantamweight	up to	119.1	54	118	53.6
Super bantamweight (Junior featherweight)	up to	–	–	122	55.4
Featherweight	up to	125.7	57	126	57.2
Super featherweight	up to	–	–	130	59
Lightweight	up to	132.3	60	135	61.2
Super lightweight (Junior welterweight)	up to	–	–	140	63.6
Light welterweight	up to	140	63.6	–	–
Welterweight	up to	147.7	67	147	66.7
Super welterweight (Junior middleweight)	up to	–	–	154	69.9
Light middleweight	up to	156.5	71	–	–
Middleweight	up to	165.4	75	160	72.6
Super middleweight	up to	–	–	168	76.2
Light heavyweight	up to	178.6	81	175	79.5
Cruiserweight – (Junior heavyweight; WBO only)	up to	–	–	190	86.2
Heavyweight	up to	200.6	91	over 190	86.2
Super heavyweight	over	200.6	91	–	–

Names in brackets are those used for the equivalent weights by WBA, IBF, and WBO

© DIAGRAM

A boxing match

WEIGH IN

On the day of the contest both boxers report to officials who weigh them to ensure that they are within the limits of their boxing weight division. They are also both given a thorough medical examination before a licence is issued allowing them to fight. In professional contests, weighing in takes place the day before, about 6pm.

STARTING THE BOUT

Before the start of a fight, the referee calls both boxers into the centre of the ring and asks them if they understand the rules of the contest (1). The boxers then shake hands and return to their corners. When the timekeeper rings his bell to indicate the beginning of the first round, both boxers advance from their corners and begin fighting.

1

DURATION OF A BOUT

Senior (open) and intermediate class amateur contests are fought over 5 rounds of 2 minutes each. Junior amateur contests are fought over 3 rounds of 2 minutes each. In professional title fights there are 12 rounds of 3 minutes each; in title eliminators, 10 or 12 rounds of 3 minutes each; and in other professional contests, 6, 8, or 10 rounds of 2 or 3 minutes each, depending on the level of experience of the contestants.

DECIDING A WINNER

There are several ways in which a boxer can win a bout.

Knockout
If one boxer is knocked to the ground, the referee orders the other into a neutral corner and begins to count out loud. If the fallen boxer gets to his feet before the referee has finished counting ten seconds, then the fight continues.

Ten-second count

©DIAGRAM

If he remains on the floor, unwilling or unable to get up, then his opponent is declared the winner. In amateur contests and some professional fights, there is a mandatory count of eight before the fight can resume.

Disqualification

The referee may disqualify either boxer if he persistently breaks the rules or commits fouls. This is very rare.

Retirement

The referee may decide at any time that one of the boxers is unfit to continue and in danger of suffering a serious or permanent injury. A boxer's seconds can also decide that he should not continue and withdraw him from the fight. A boxer cannot overrule this decision, even if he feels he is fit enough to continue.

Points

If, after the full number of rounds has been fought, neither boxer has been knocked out, disqualified or retired, then the bout is decided on points.

Throughout the fight judges award points at the end of each round. The boxer judged to have won a round is awarded maximum points (20 in amateur bouts and 10 in professional), his opponent is awarded less points depending on his performance. If a round is judged to be a draw, then both are awarded full points.

In amateur contests additional points are also awarded for the number of good punches made (punches which strike the target area with the knuckle part of the glove). A point is awarded for every 3 good punches. At the end of an amateur bout in which all points are equal the boxer who is judged to have attacked the most is declared the winner. Amateur bouts are never declared draws.

Winning

In professional contests additional points can be awarded for attacking skills, defending skills and overall style. If points are equal at the end of a fight the contest may be declared a draw.

Fighting techniques

OUTFIGHTING

Outfighting is the term applied to the techniques used by boxers at a distance from each other. These include arm's-length punches and agile footwork. Skilful boxers concentrate on their outfighting techniques because they offer the best opportunities to tire and attack an opponent while minimising opportunities for counterattack. (The following fighting techniques apply to right-handed boxers.)

Basic stance

This is the position from which all attacking and defensive moves begin. It combines balance, defence and readiness. A good basic stance is absolutely essential.

Stand with your legs apart and with the left leg further forward than the right. Your weight should be evenly distributed to provide a firm, balanced base. Your right heel should be slightly raised and your left leg flexed so that you are ready to move quickly. Tuck your elbows in close to your body so that your upper arms shield both sides of your chest. Hold your left glove out at shoulder height, loosely clenched and with the thumb uppermost. It should be far enough out to allow a quick attacking punch, but close enough to be quickly drawn back for defence. Hold your right glove underneath your chin with the wrist towards you. From this position it is ready to defend your head but also to deliver a powerful punch with your full bodyweight behind it.

Footwork

Agile footwork is vital. You must be light on your feet so that you can stay out of trouble and get into an attacking position when the time is right. You also need to be balanced at all times or you could easily be knocked to the floor. To maintain good balance, keep your feet apart as you move and never cross your legs. Move the foot closest to the direction in which you want to move first, and then bring the other foot after it.

Punching

To be really effective an arm's-length punch needs your whole bodyweight behind it. Twist your body into the punch and extend your arm as hard and fast as possible. Imagine that you are punching through the target (see over).

Straight left

This is the best way to force an opponent to keep his distance. From the basic stance simply straighten your left arm and turn your hips and shoulders into the blow. Your fist will automatically twist so the knuckles are uppermost just before impact. If you have room, slide your left foot forward for the blow, but remember to quickly bring up your right foot to recover your balance.

Left hook

From the basic stance twist your body sharply to the left at the waist, shifting your weight onto your right foot. Bring your left elbow up, keeping the wrist rigid with the arm, otherwise there is a chance of snapping your wrist. Pull the fist round into your opponent's side. Hooks can also be made with the right arm.

Uppercut

These are upward blows to your opponent's chin or body. They can be delivered with the left or right hand. To make a right uppercut, transfer your weight onto your right foot and twist your shoulders and hips hard to the left, bringing your right forearm up into the target. Try not to lean back as you do this or you will be dangerously off balance.

Straight right

This is the most powerful and damaging punch, but it is
tiring and may leave you open to counterattack if you
miss or if it is successfully blocked. Twist your waist and
shoulders into the punch and straighten your right arm so
that it is at full stretch just as the blow impacts. If there is
room, you can also lean your bodyweight forward onto
your left foot.

INFIGHTING

Infighting is the term applied to techniques used at close quarters. It makes greater demands on a boxer's sheer strength and endurance than the more skilful techniques of outfighting since it inevitably involves receiving blows as well as giving them. It is, however, the nature of the sport that hard infighting is an important part of any serious bout.

Getting in close

The best way to get in close to your opponent is to parry or sidestep a straight left and then move inside his extended left arm (**1**). Keep your guard well up and crouch slightly as you move in. Try to keep both of your opponent's arms outside of your own (**2**).

Punches

Close-quarter punches are not very powerful but can be delivered in rapid succession and in a variety of combinations. They can sap your opponent's strength and throw him onto the defensive. Use short hooks (**3**) and uppercuts (**4**) (**see over**).

Breaking away

The great trick to learn when it comes to infighting is how to get out of it! Ideally you should be able to get in close to your opponent, deliver a quick succession of blows, and then move out to arm's length before suffering too much damage yourself. To break away from an infighting situation, put your gloves on your opponent's arms and push yourself backwards (**5**); this has the

advantage of preventing him from delivering any punches as you move back. Another method is to sidestep, letting your opponent's momentum carry him forwards, then turn him away from you with your right hand and push yourself away with your left (**6**).

Clinches

During infighting, and particularly when boxers are becoming tired, arms can get tangled up so that nobody can deliver a punch. This is called a clinch (**7**). When this happens, the referee will call 'break!' and both boxers must let go and take one pace backwards. It is a foul to hit your opponent on the break (**8**).

7   8

DEFENCE

Good defensive skills are just as important as good attacking skills. It is no good delivering devastating punches if they just leave you wide open to counterattack, particularly if your opponent is avoiding most of the damage from your blows with his own defence. Agility and lightning reflexes are the pre-requisites for defence.

A good boxer will also be able to anticipate his opponent's next attack. A large part of a fight may be won by simply avoiding your opponent's punches and tiring him out with the wasted effort.

There are several ways to defend yourself from a punch:
1 Sidestep
2 Snap back
3 Sway to one side
4 Stop the punch with your forearm, shoulder or elbow

5 Stop the punch with your glove
6 Duck down
7 Parry, or deflect to one side
8 Cover up

© DIAGRAM

COUNTERING

It is not enough just to avoid or deflect an opponent's punches, you must be ready to strike back in the best way. A boxer's real talent shows itself in his countering skills; he must think on his feet and respond to every opportunity that presents itself with flair and imagination.

The straight left is the punch you will face most often so it is vital that you know how to deal with it. Here are a few classic tactics.

Straight left counters

Block your opponent's left with your right glove and return a straight left to his chin (**1**).

Duck beneath your opponent's left and return a straight left to his body (**2**).

Straight right counters

Duck inside your opponent's left so that it passes over your left shoulder then throw a straight right to his head (**3**), twist from the hips to get your full weight into it.

Sidestep to the left and throw a straight right to his head just inside your opponent's left arm (**4**).

Other counters

Parry his left over your right shoulder, pivot sharply to the right and throw a left hook at his chin (**5**).

© DIAGRAM

Sidestep right and slip outside his left, then twist back round to the left and deliver a right uppercut to his body (**6**) (See previous page).

COUNTERING A SOUTHPAW

A southpaw is a boxer whose basic stance is with the right arm extended, a mirror image of the normal stance. Southpaws are usually left-handed, so their strongest punch is the straight left. When facing a southpaw a conventional boxer must remember to keep up his right guard and to avoid moving to the right. He must also remember that the southpaw has the advantage of being used to facing conventional boxers' tactics.

Southpaw tactics
You lead with a straight left. The southpaw sidesteps to his left, and replies with a straight right to your chin (**1**). You lead with a straight left. The southpaw ducks and sways right, hitting you with a left to your body (**2**).

Counter tactics

If the southpaw leads with a straight right, here are three ways to reply.

1 Parry his right, and counter with a straight right to the chin.
2 Slip inside his right, and reply with a left hook over his right arm.
3 Duck under his right (**a**) and follow up with a right to his body (**b**).

Training techniques

Boxing places great physical demands on the body. A boxer needs to have a very high level of general fitness; this can only be achieved through regular training, a strict diet and a healthy lifestyle. Smoking, drugs, excessive drinking and irregular sleep must all be avoided, which can put difficult restrictions on a young person's social life. At professional level, boxers must dedicate virtually their whole lives to keeping fit and perfecting their skills.

GENERAL FITNESS

Over the years, boxers have developed a set of basic training techniques which are particularly good at promoting general fitness and developing the strength and agility needed for their sport.

1 Roadwork A regular run of up to 8km (5 miles) a day is an excellent way to develop stamina, good respiration and a strong heart.
2 Jogging on the spot A basic exercise which toughens leg muscles and promotes good balance.
3 Push ups Another simple exercise which toughens arm muscles and develops upper body strength.
4 Skipping An excellent way to develop stamina, strengthen the leg muscles and also develop agility.
5 Static cycling Very good for overall fitness.
6 Rowing machines Very good for overall fitness.

FIGHTING TRAINING TECHNIQUES

Other techniques are used to develop specific
boxing skills.

Shadow boxing A technique in which a boxer pretends
to box against himself in front of a mirror. This helps to
develop quick thinking and fast reflexes.

Punchbags and punchballs are used to develop
punching strength and control. Large, heavy punchbags
suspended from the ceiling help boxers learn how to put
their full weight into a punch. Small, inflatable punch
balls on springy mounts are used to develop hand-eye
coordination and timing.

Punchbags and punchballs

SPARRING

One of the best ways to train and develop fighting skills
is to practise with a sparring partner. Sparring is just like
a real boxing match except that the boxers do not use
their full strength when punching. They also wear added
protection. Sparring is an excellent way of learning how
to cope with different boxing styles.

A good skill to practise when sparring is how to dominate
the boxing ring. By keeping to the centre and making
your opponent move as much as possible, you will tire
him out and also have the psychological advantage of
seeming to be in control of the fight.

Dominating the ring – practice

Sparring equipment

Boxers wear special protective equipment when sparring to reduce the risk of injuring themselves before a genuine contest.

1 **Headguard** protects the head and face from heavy punches.

2 **Foul protector** defends the abdomen and groin area from accidental foul punches.

3 **Padded gloves** lessen the impact of punches.

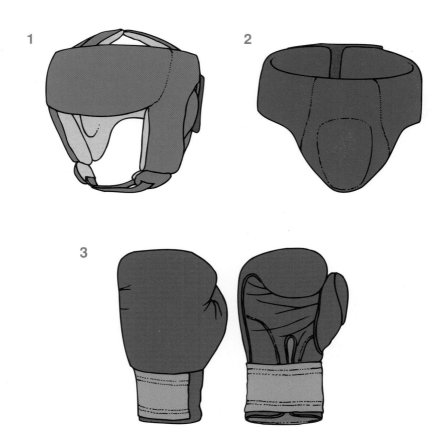

Glossary

Break	Referee's command to boxers to withdraw from a clinch.
Butting	Illegal use of head to hit opponent.
Clinch	Position in which the contestants' arms become intertwined.
Count	Count by referee from 1 to 10 that takes place when boxer has been knocked to the floor of the ring or is lying through or helpless on the ropes.
Count-out	Defeat of boxer through his failure to rise by the count of 10.
Counter	Punch made after successful avoidance of an opponent's punch.
Foul protector	Guard worn by boxers around groin during sparring practice.
Guard	Defensive position adopted by boxers to shield themselves from an opponent's blows.
Gumshield	Piece of plastic clenched in the mouth during a fight to protect the teeth and prevent the tongue being bitten.
Headguard	Head protector used by boxers during sparring practice.
Hook	Sideways blow delivered (by either hand) with elbow in hooked position.

Infighting	Those parts of a bout during which contestants fight close up to one another.
Jab	Quick punch that does not have the boxer's full weight behind it.
Knock-out blow	Blow that knocks a boxer unconscious.
Outfighting	Those parts of a bout during which the contestants remain at arm's length from one another.
Parry	Deflection of an opponent's punch with glove or arm.
Points	Score given to a boxer for his performance during a fight. Used to decide the result if the bout ends without a count-out, disqualification, etc.
Queensberry Rules	The first official rules of boxing, laid down by the Marquess of Queensberry in 1865.
Round	A fighting period, lasting two or three minutes. Any bout is divided into a number of these, with one-minute rest intervals in between.
Second	Attendant who escorts boxer to ring and advises and tends him between rounds.
Shadow-boxing	Training technique in which the boxer practises on his own.

Southpaw	Left-handed boxer.
Slip	Sideways movement to avoid a punch.
Snap back	Sudden swaying of body backward, to avoid a punch.
Sparring	Training sessions or fights with a partner.
Straight left	Blow delivered with left fist, arm outstretched.
Straight right	Blow delivered with right fist, arm outstretched.
Uppercut	Upward-moving blow (from either hand) delivered with the larger knuckles.
Weigh in	Ceremony at which contestants are weighed, to ensure that they are within the limits for their division.